DOGS AND CATS WITH TATTOOS

THIS BOOK BELONGS TO:

_____

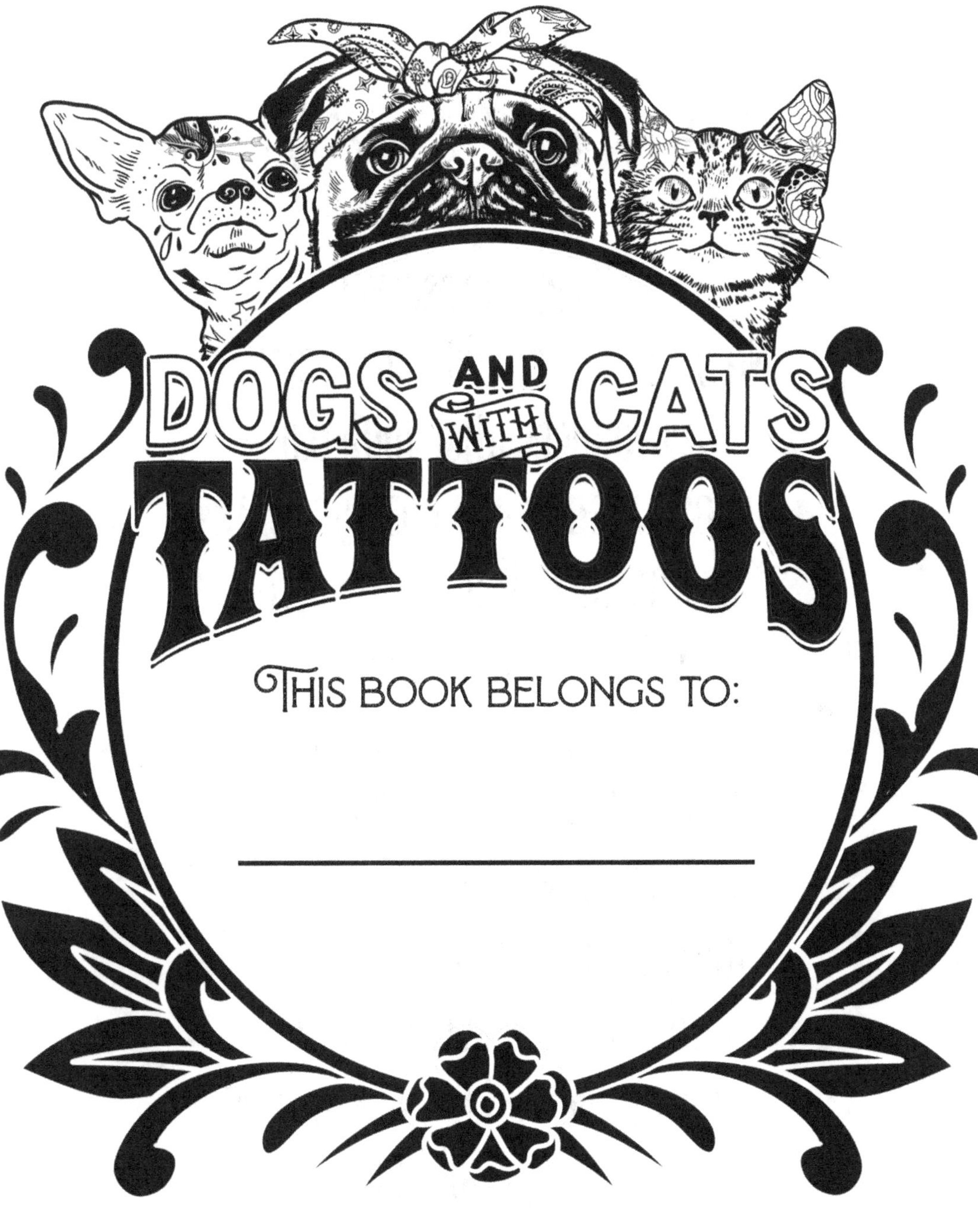

Copyright © 2020

All rights reserved.
No part of this publication may be reproduced, distributed,or transmitted in any form or by any means, including photocoying, recording, or other electronic or mechanical methods, without the prior written permission of the publisher, except in the case of brief quotations embodied in critical reviews and certain other noncommercial uses permitted by copyright law.

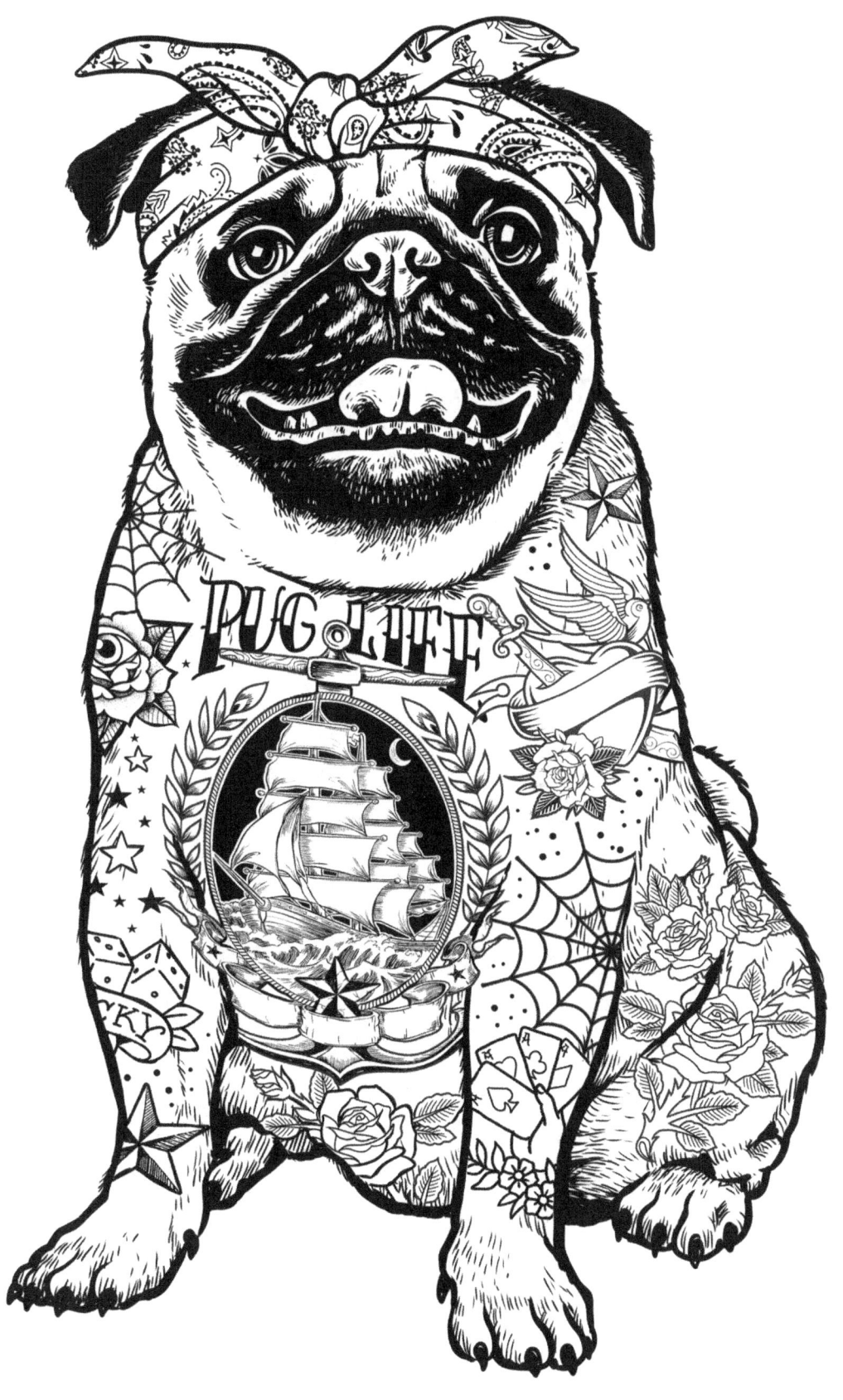

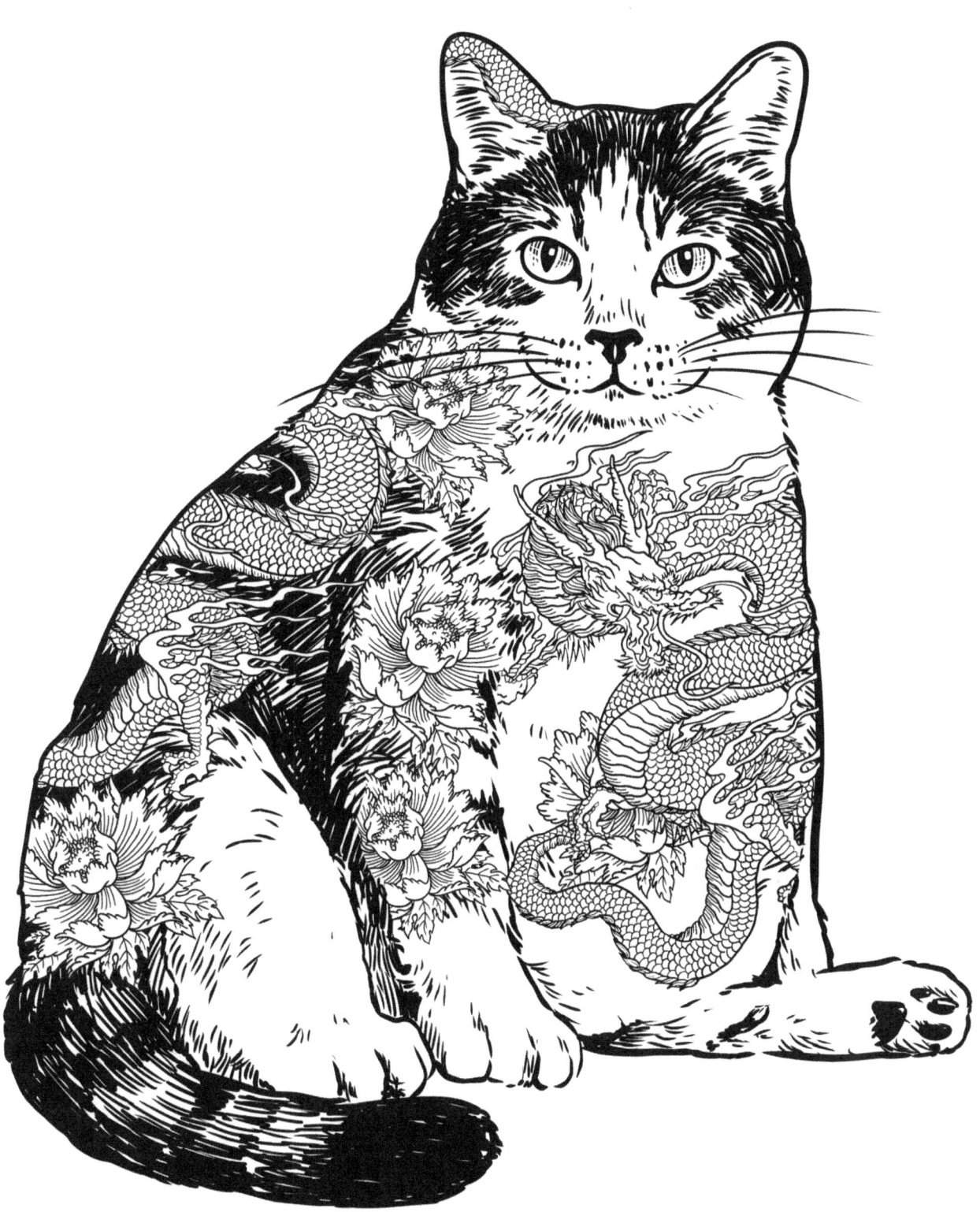

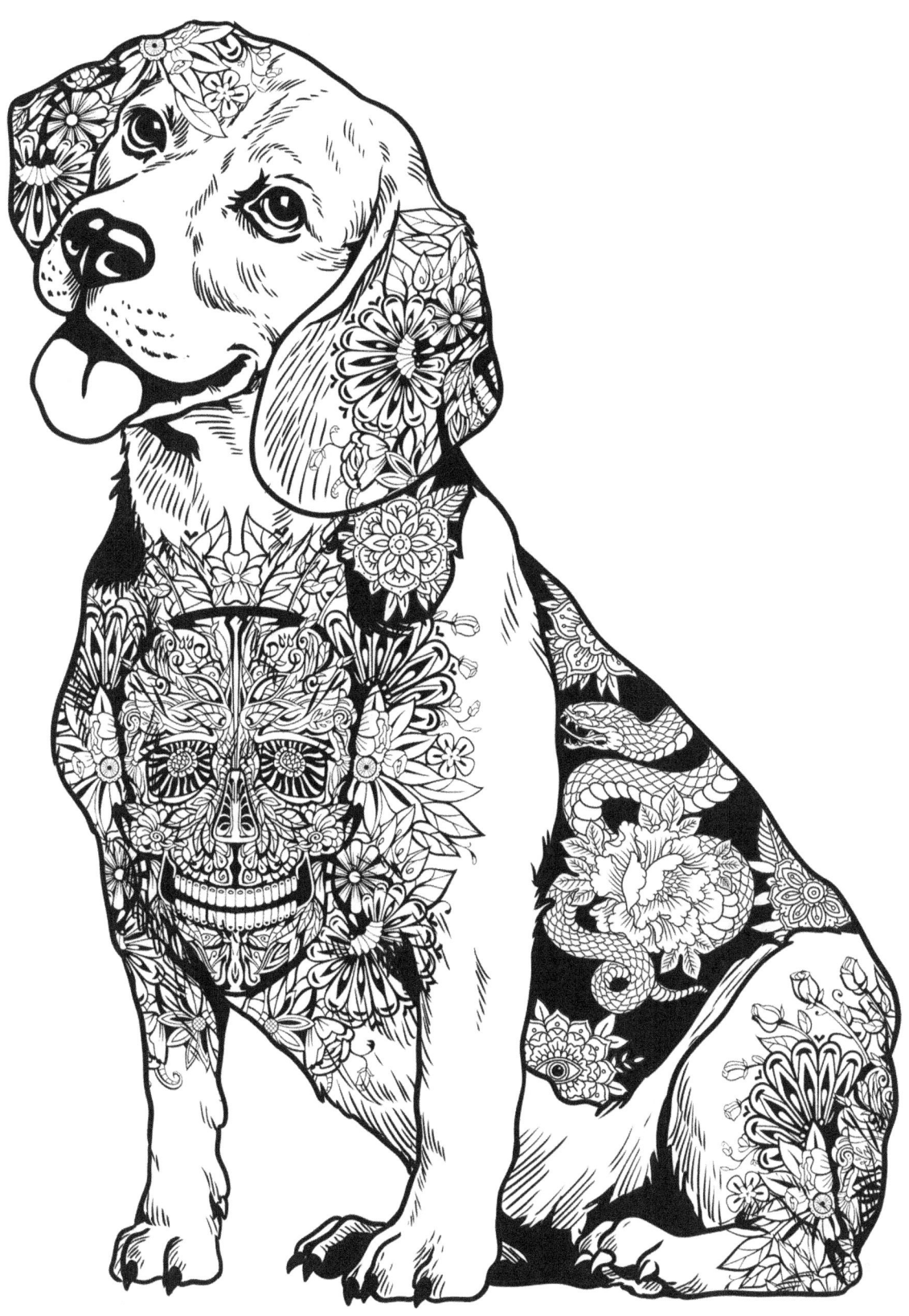

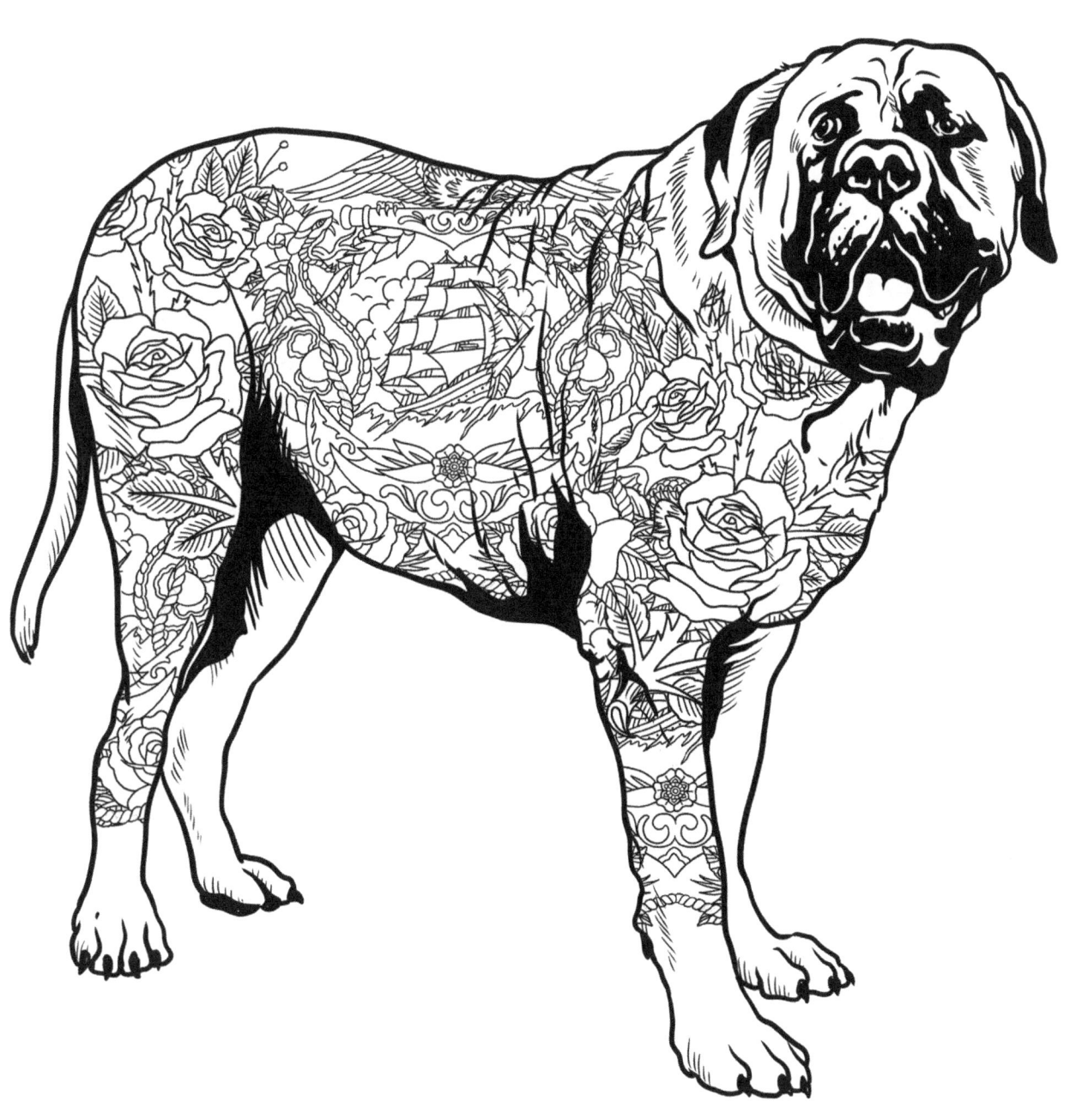

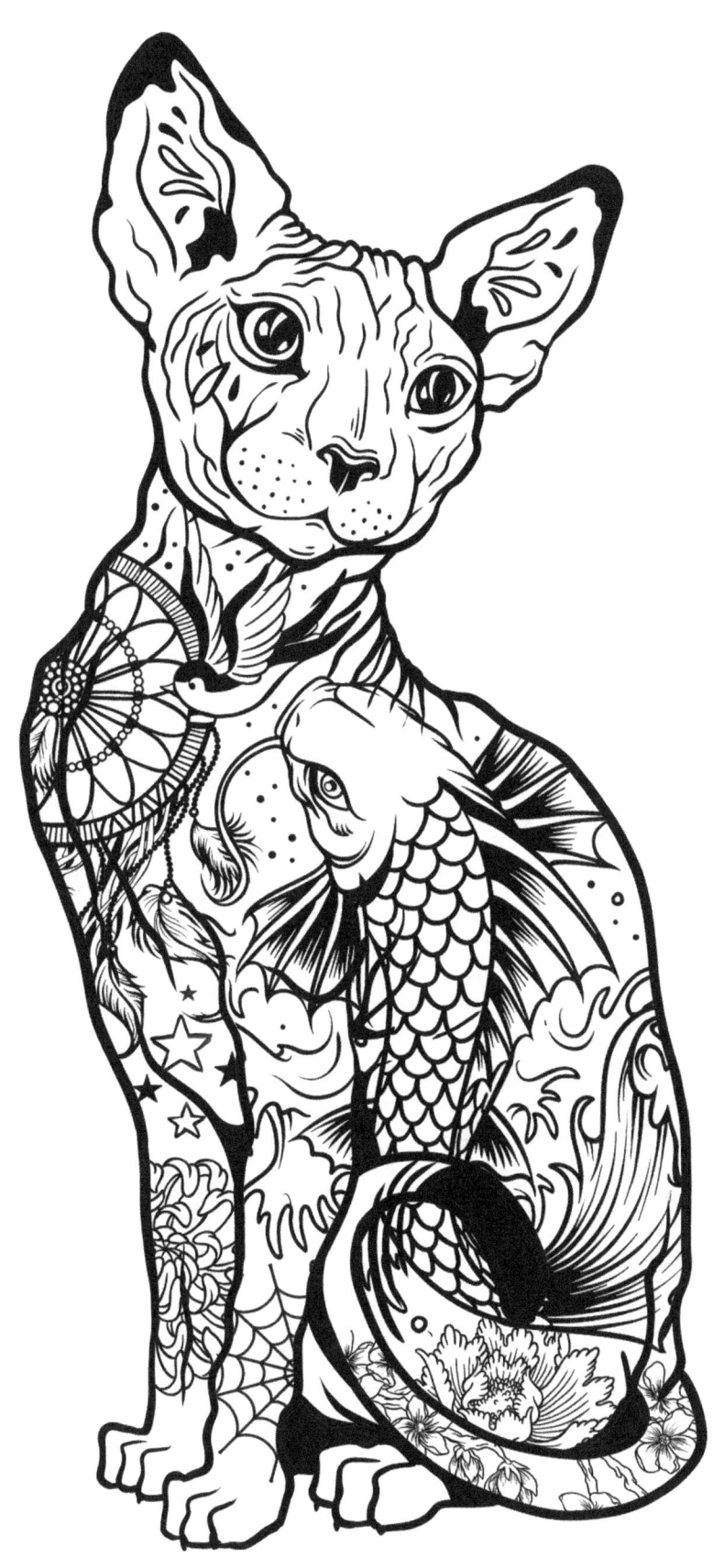

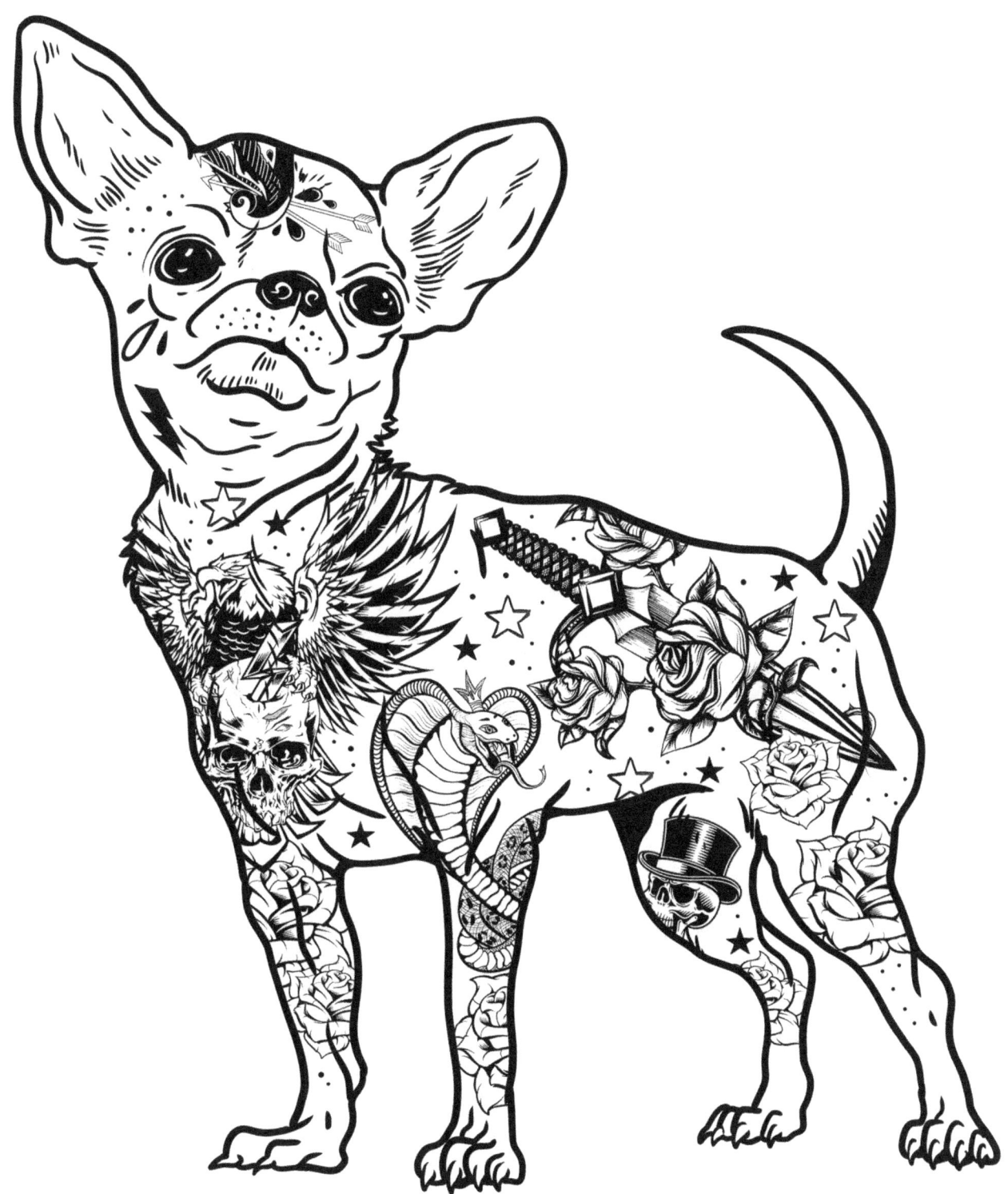

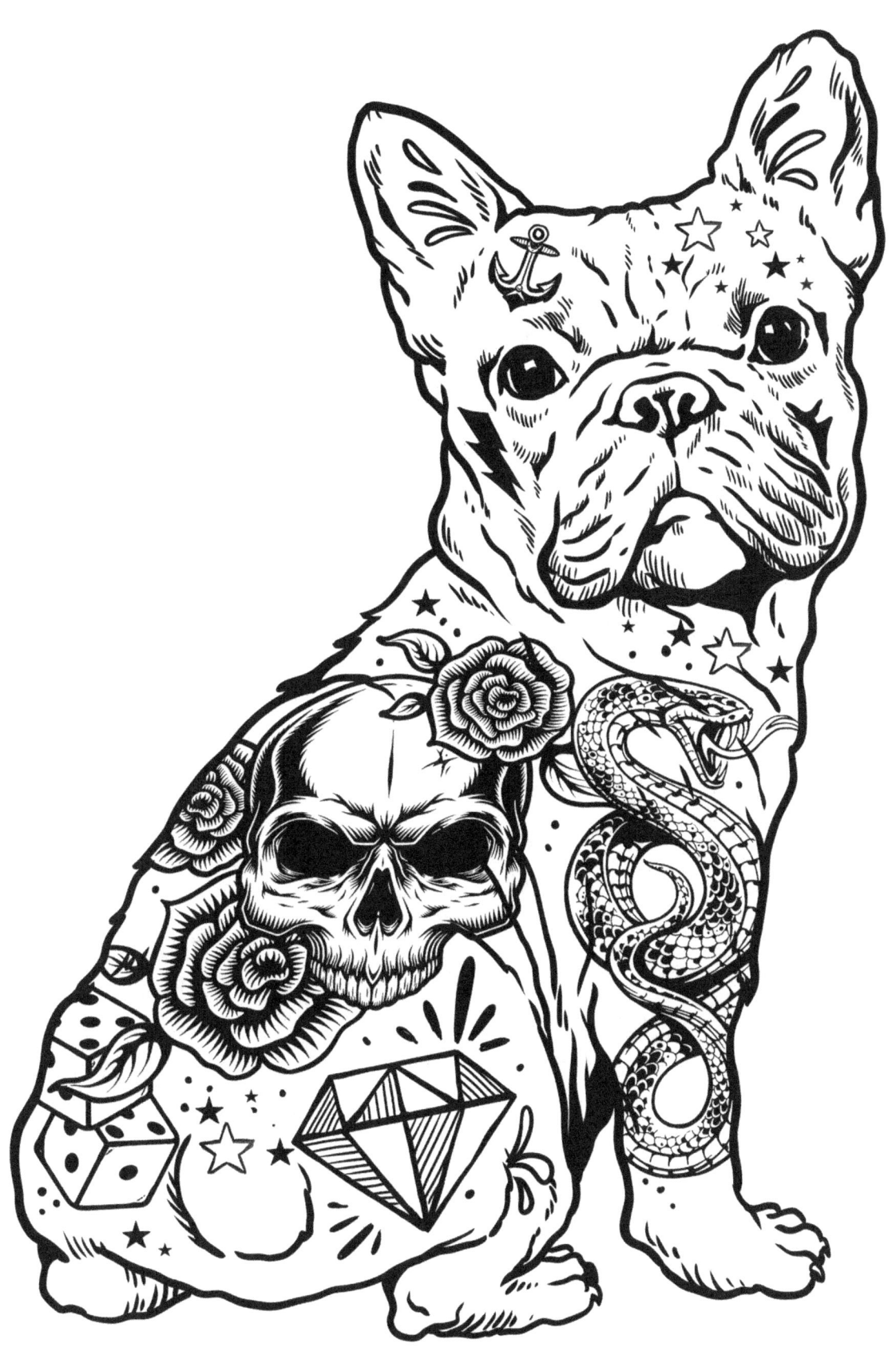

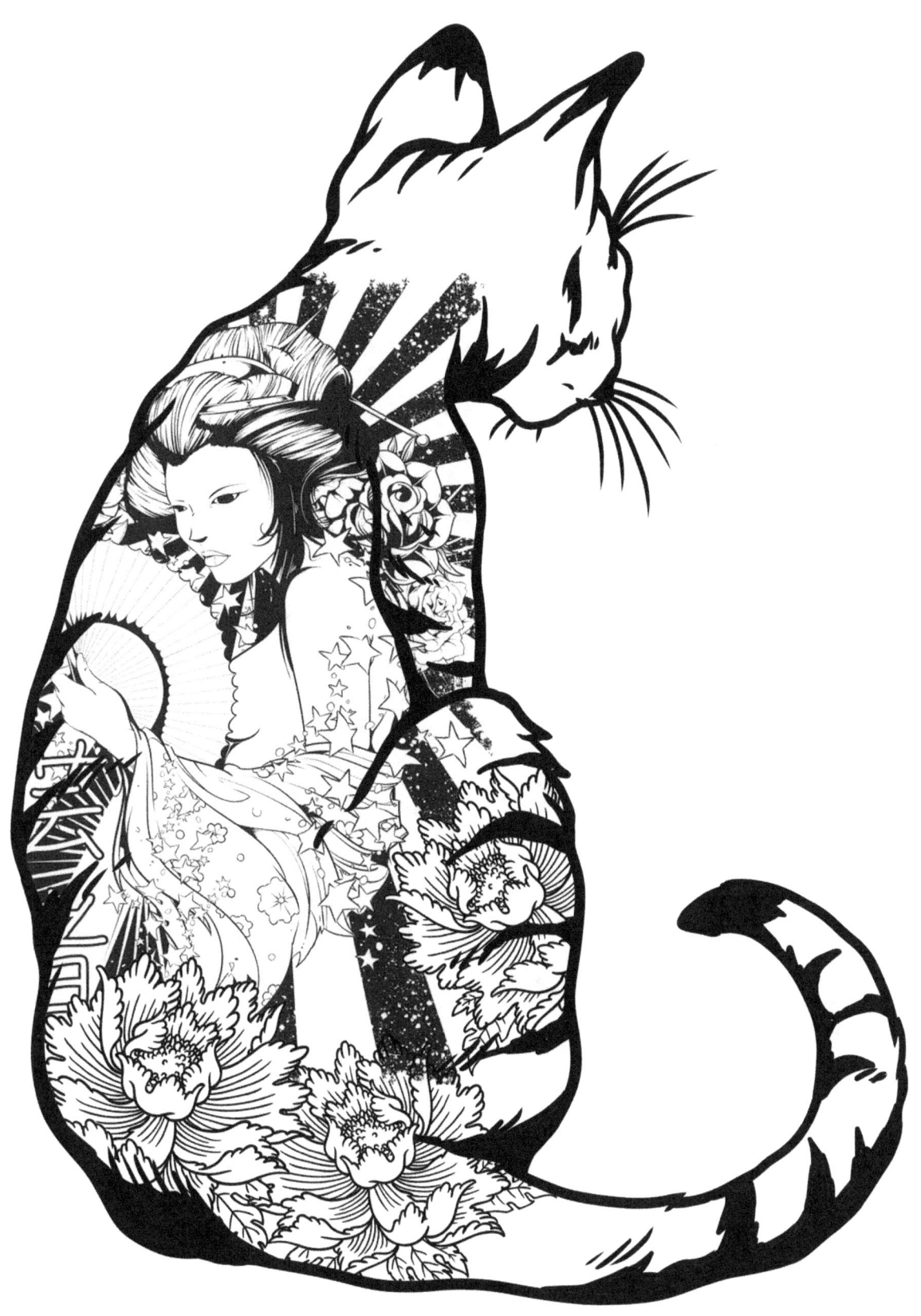

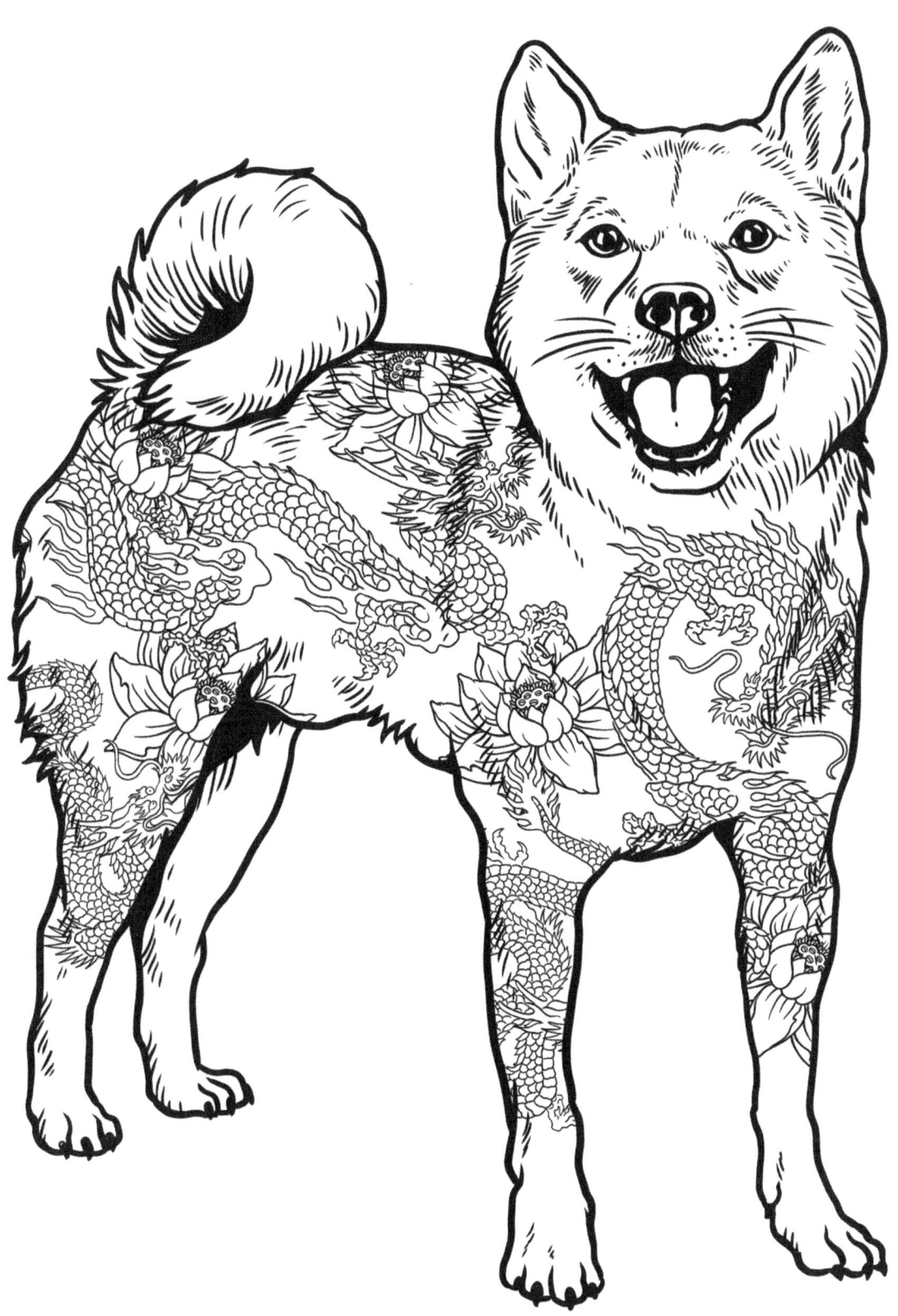

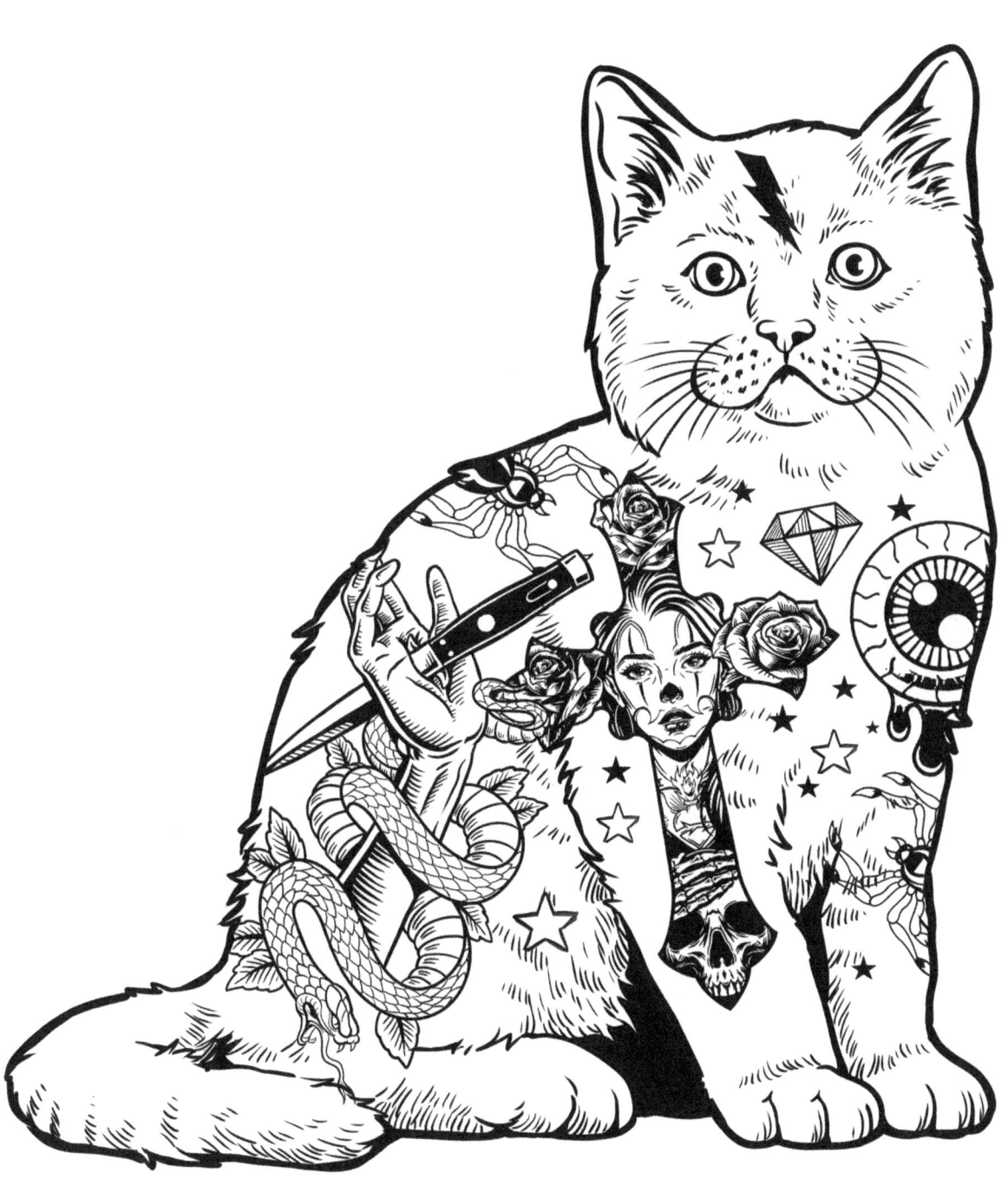

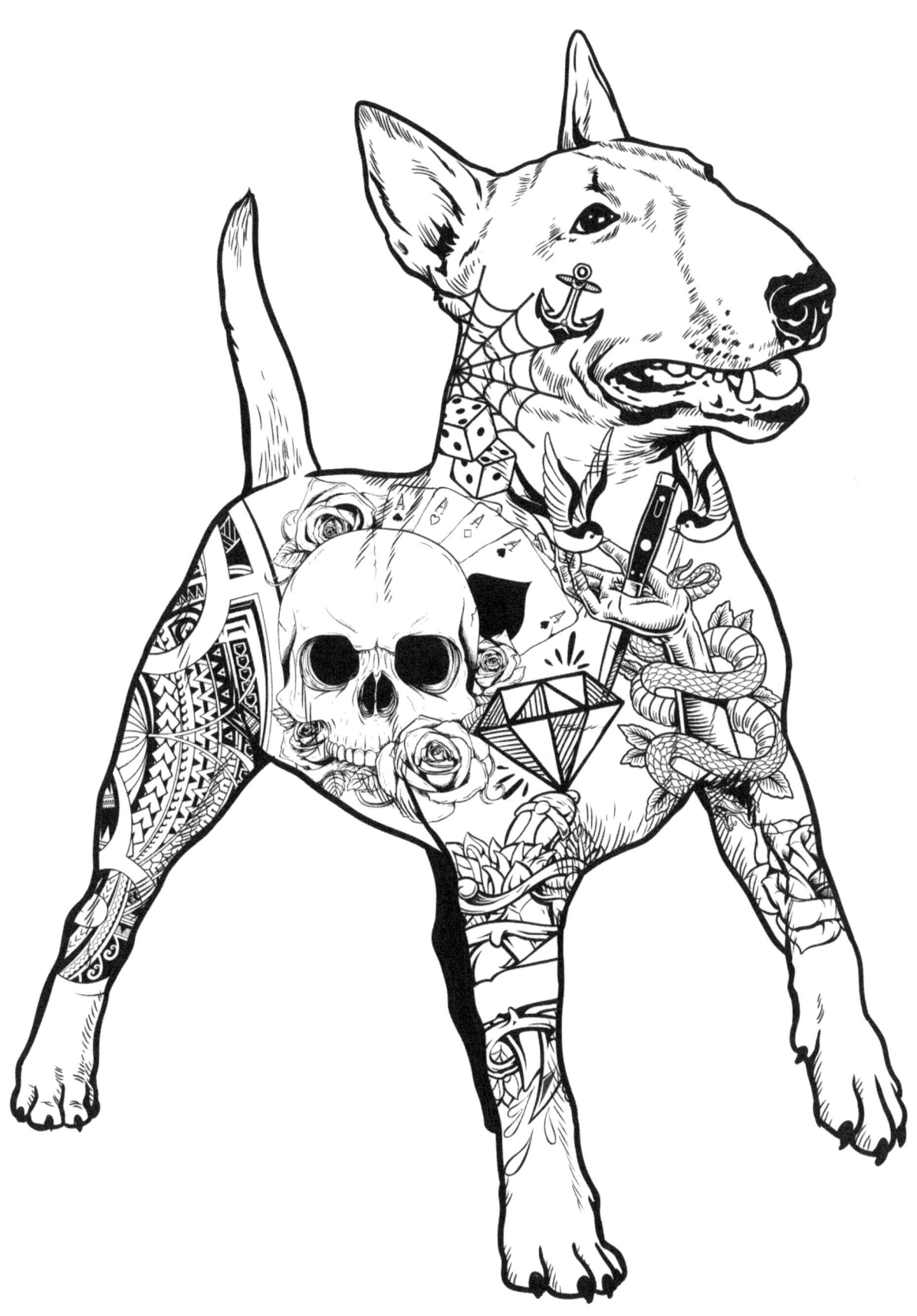

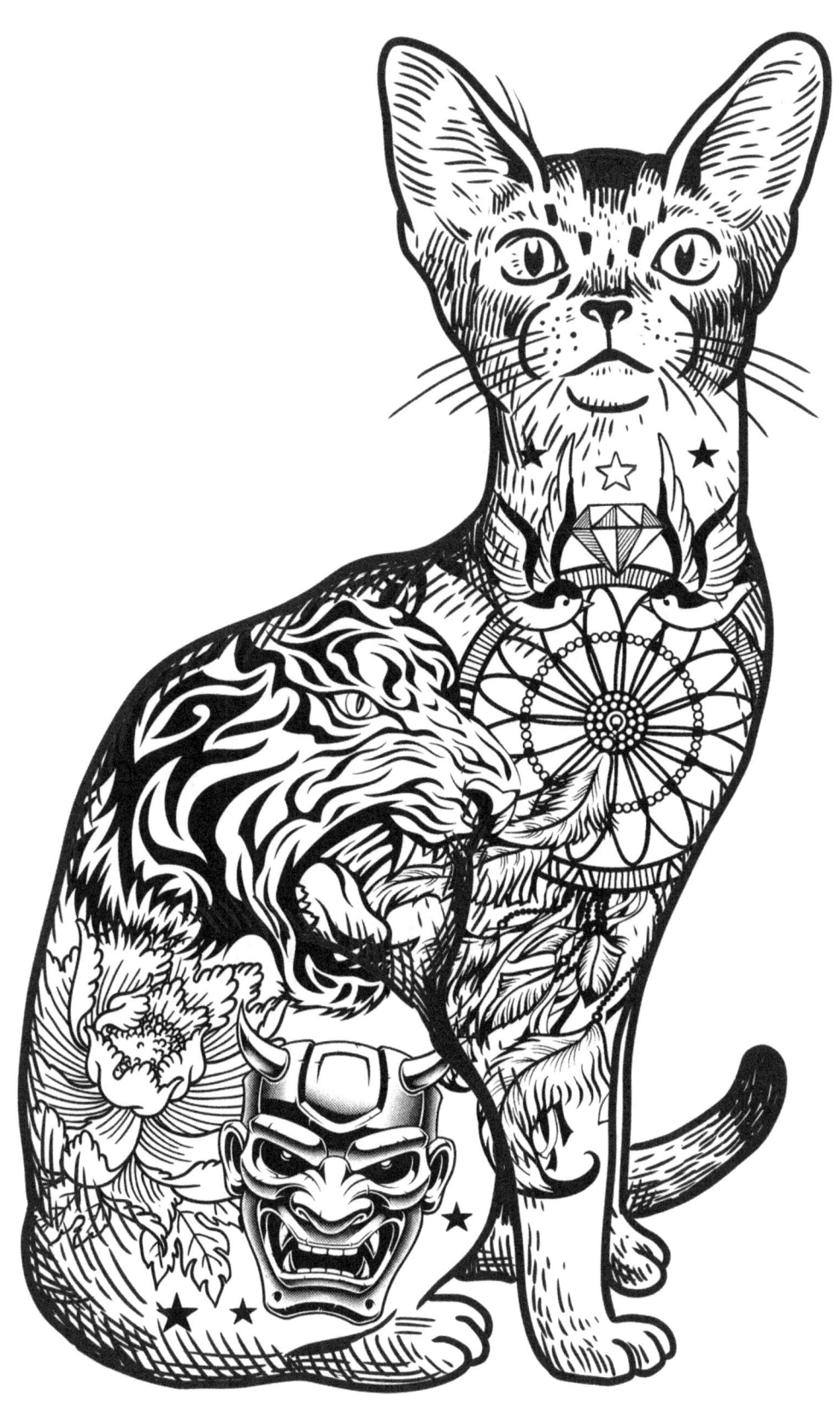

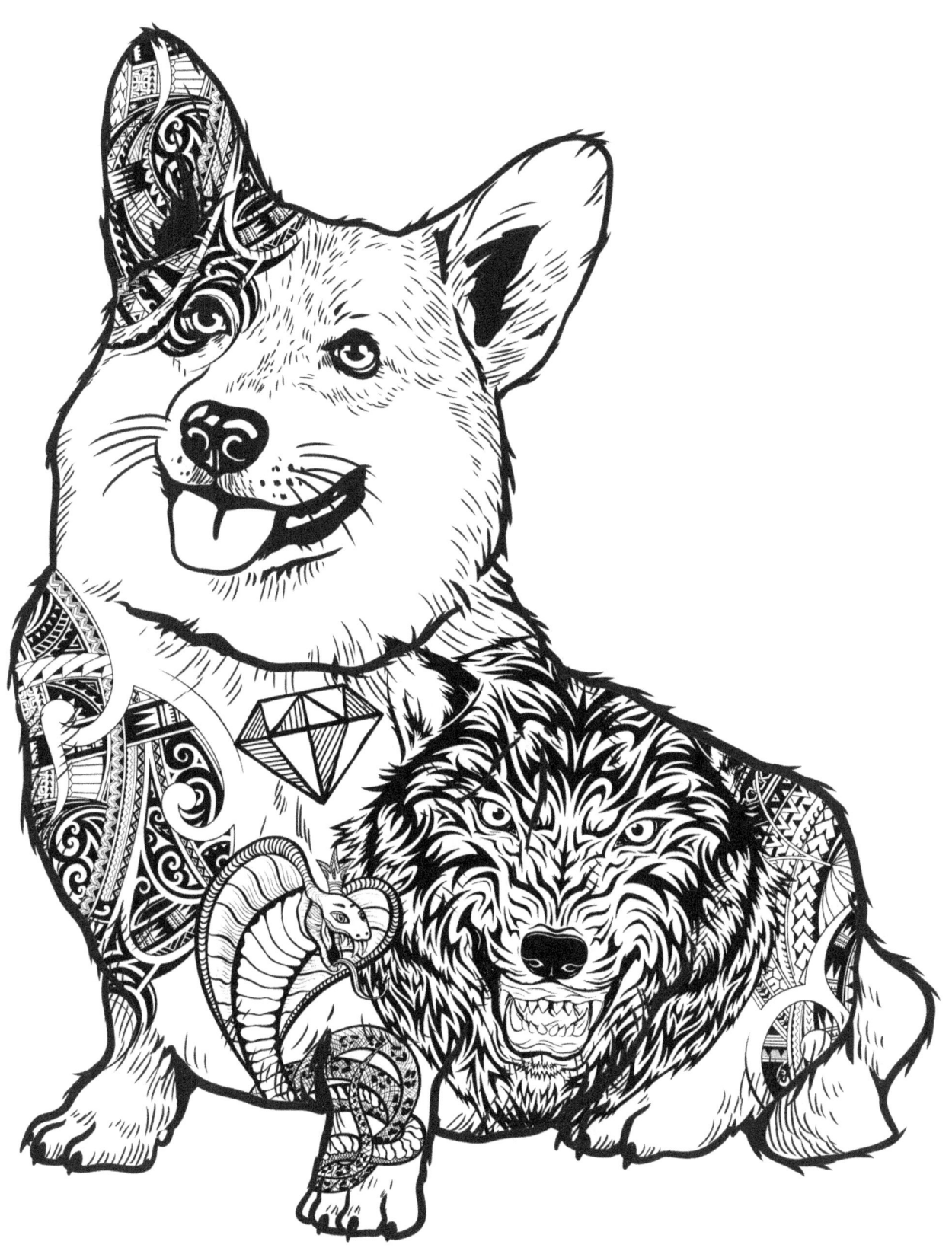

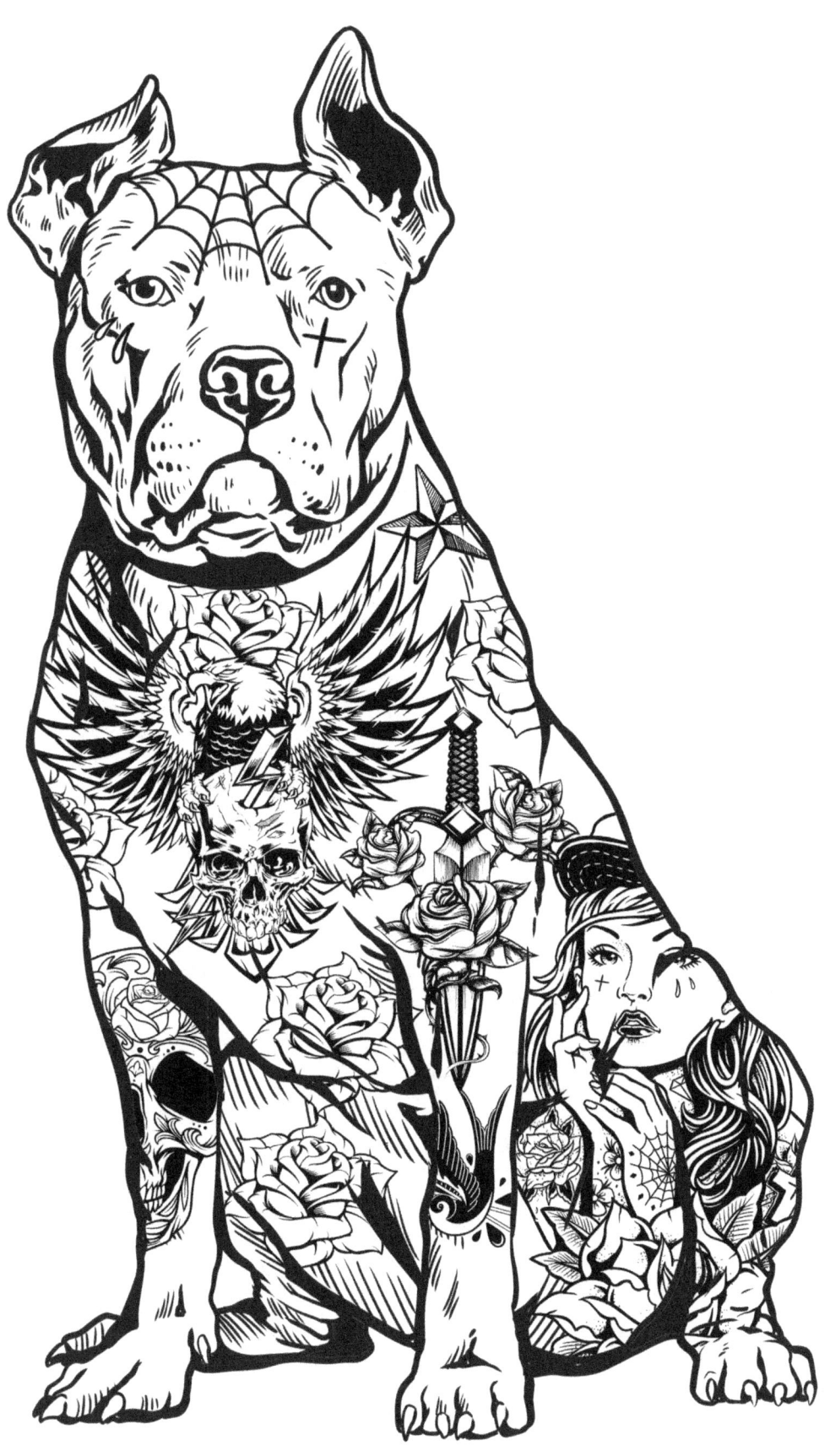

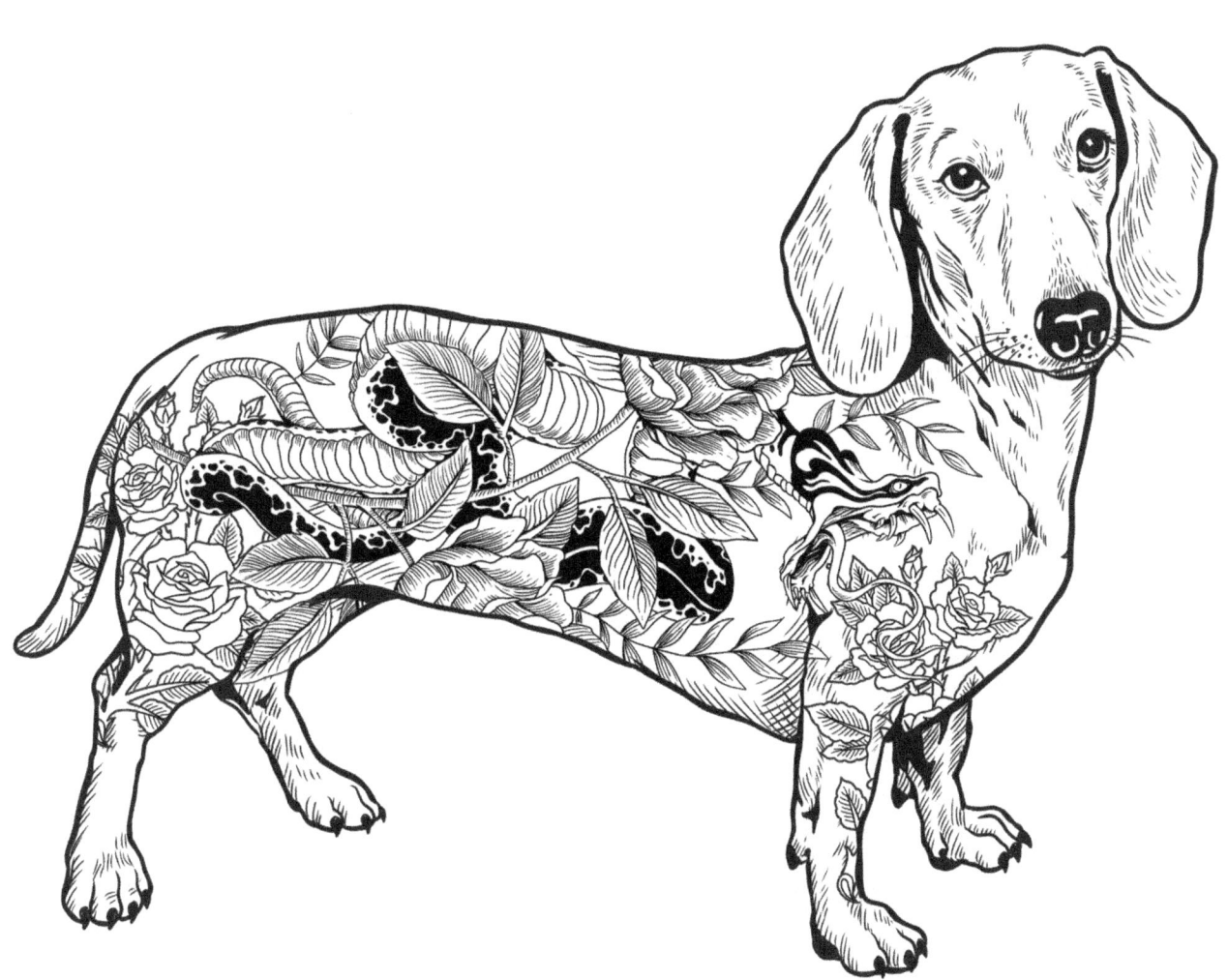

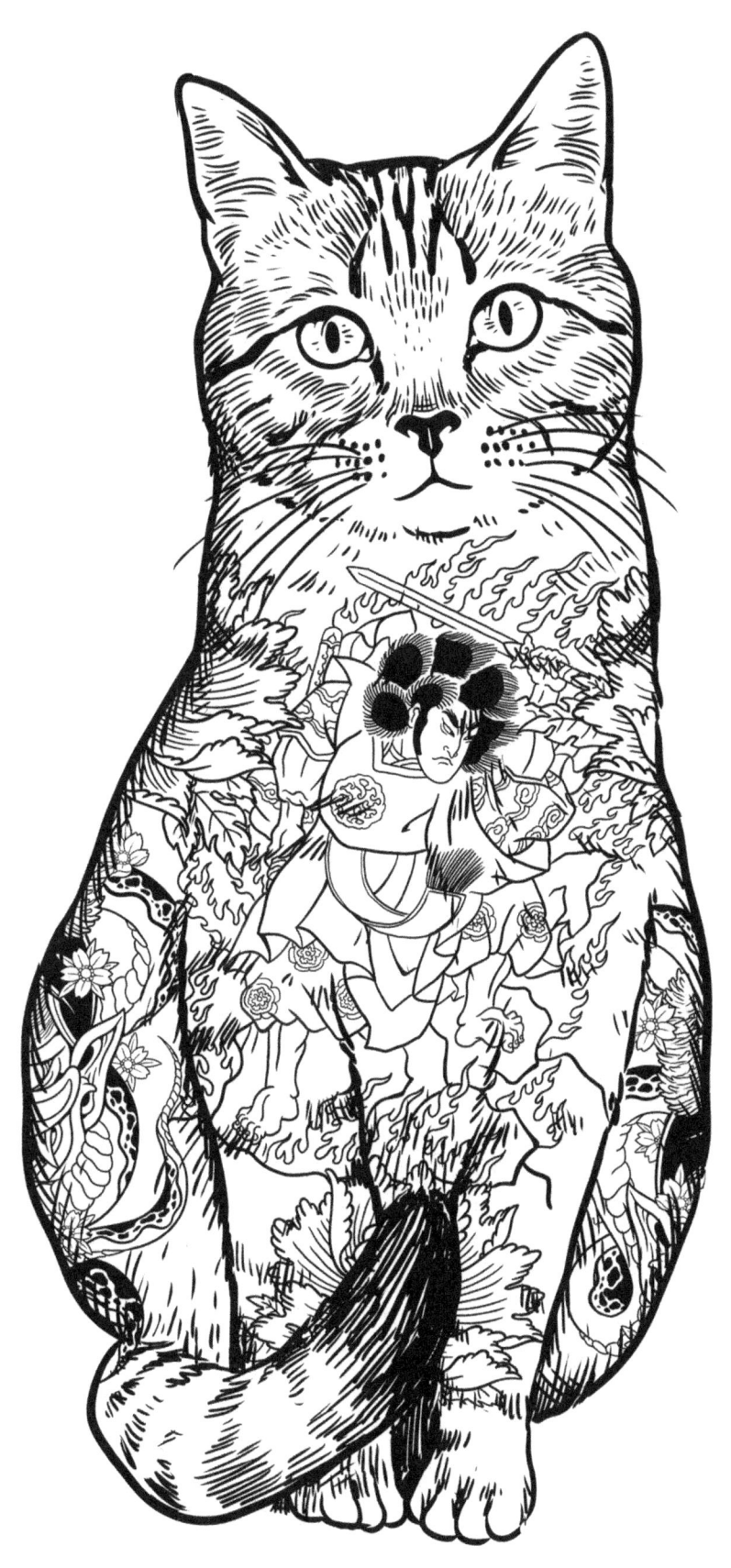

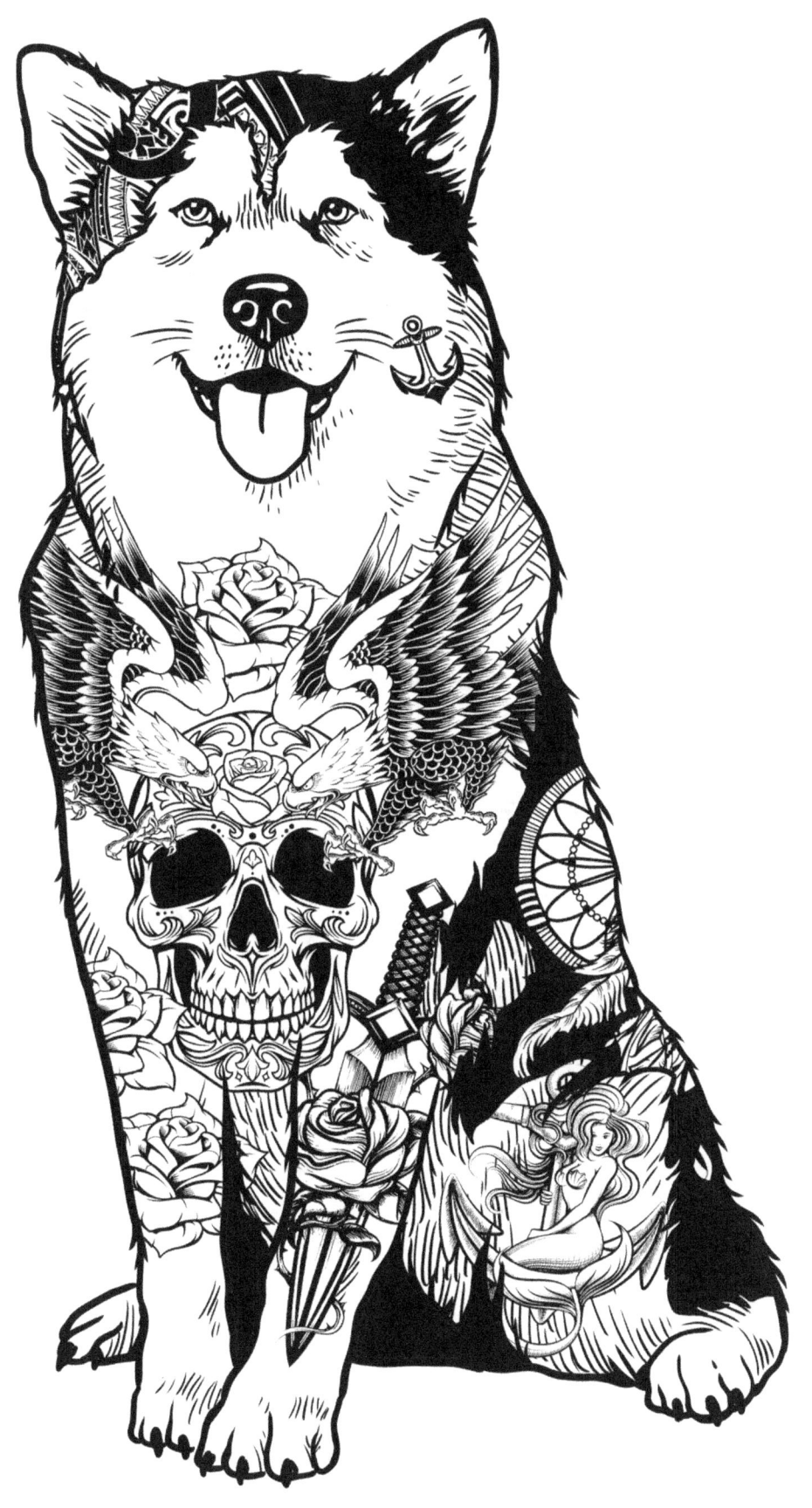

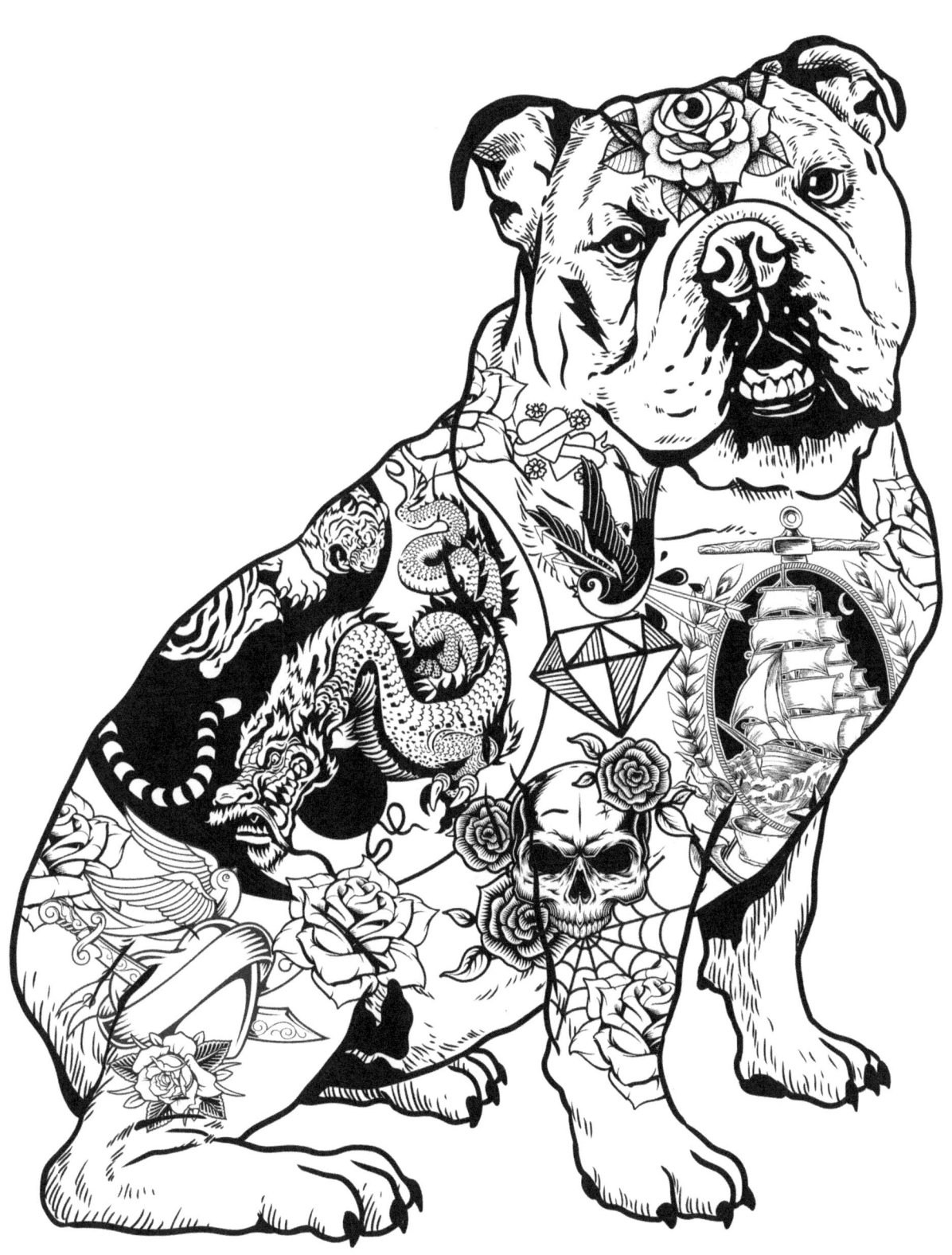

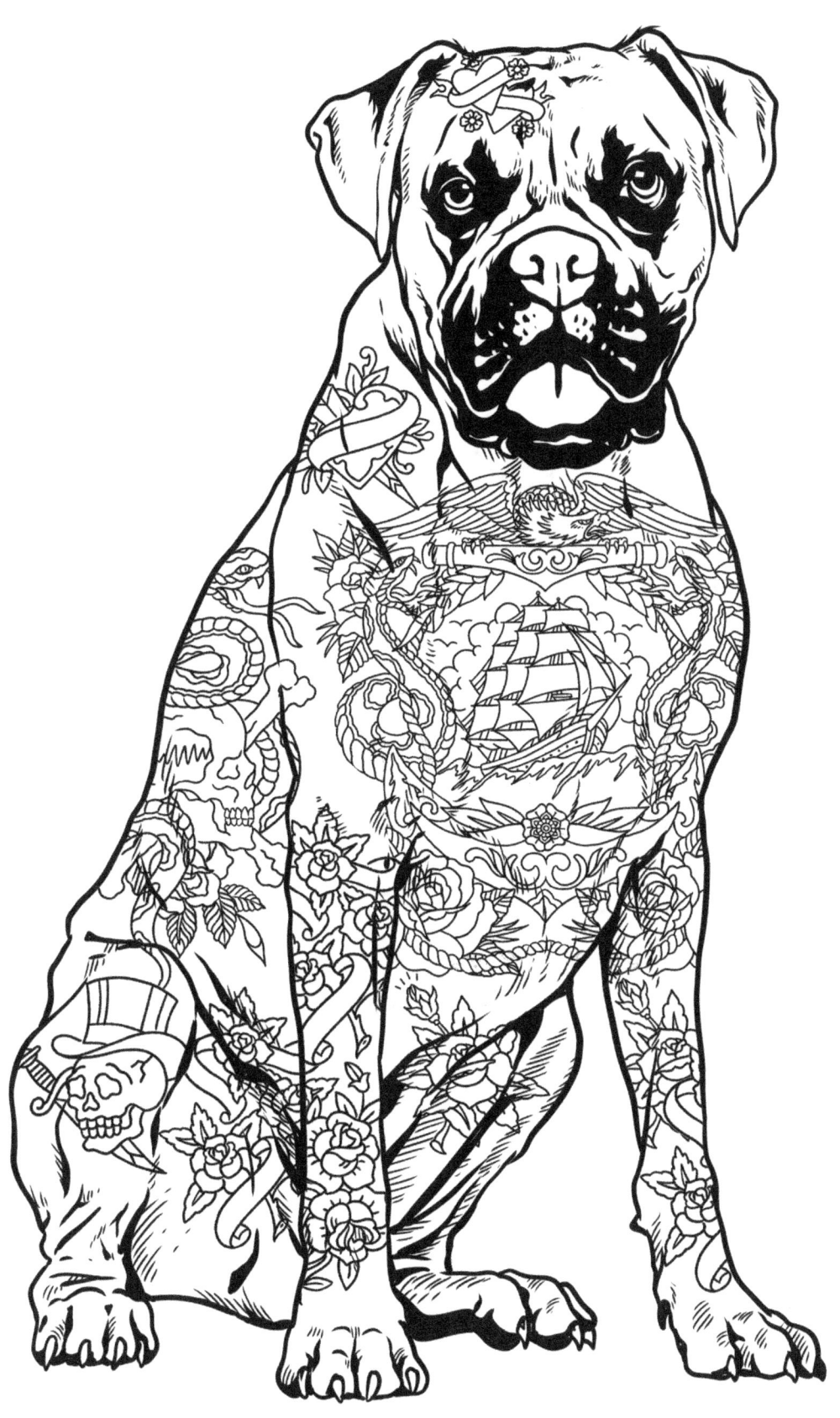

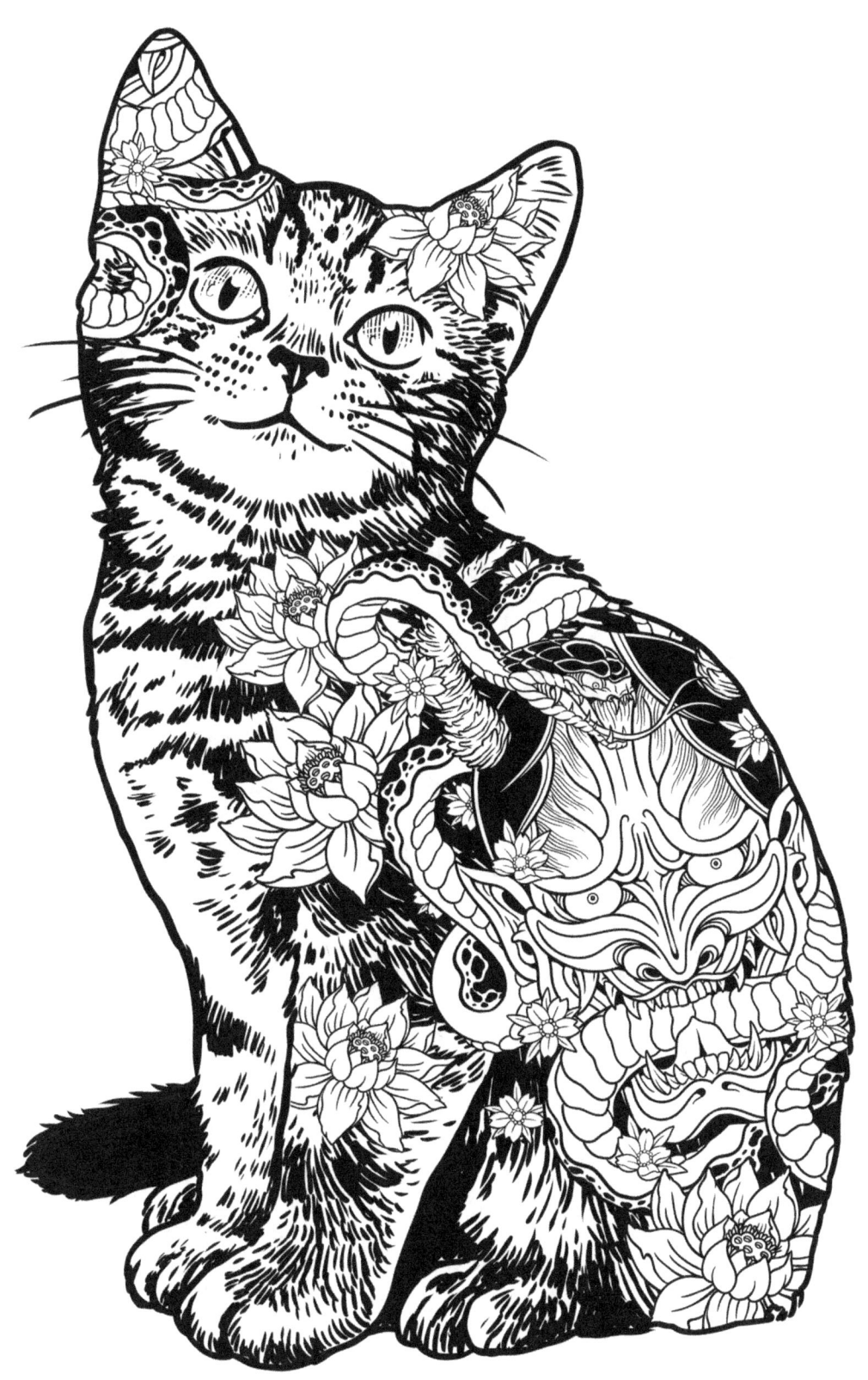

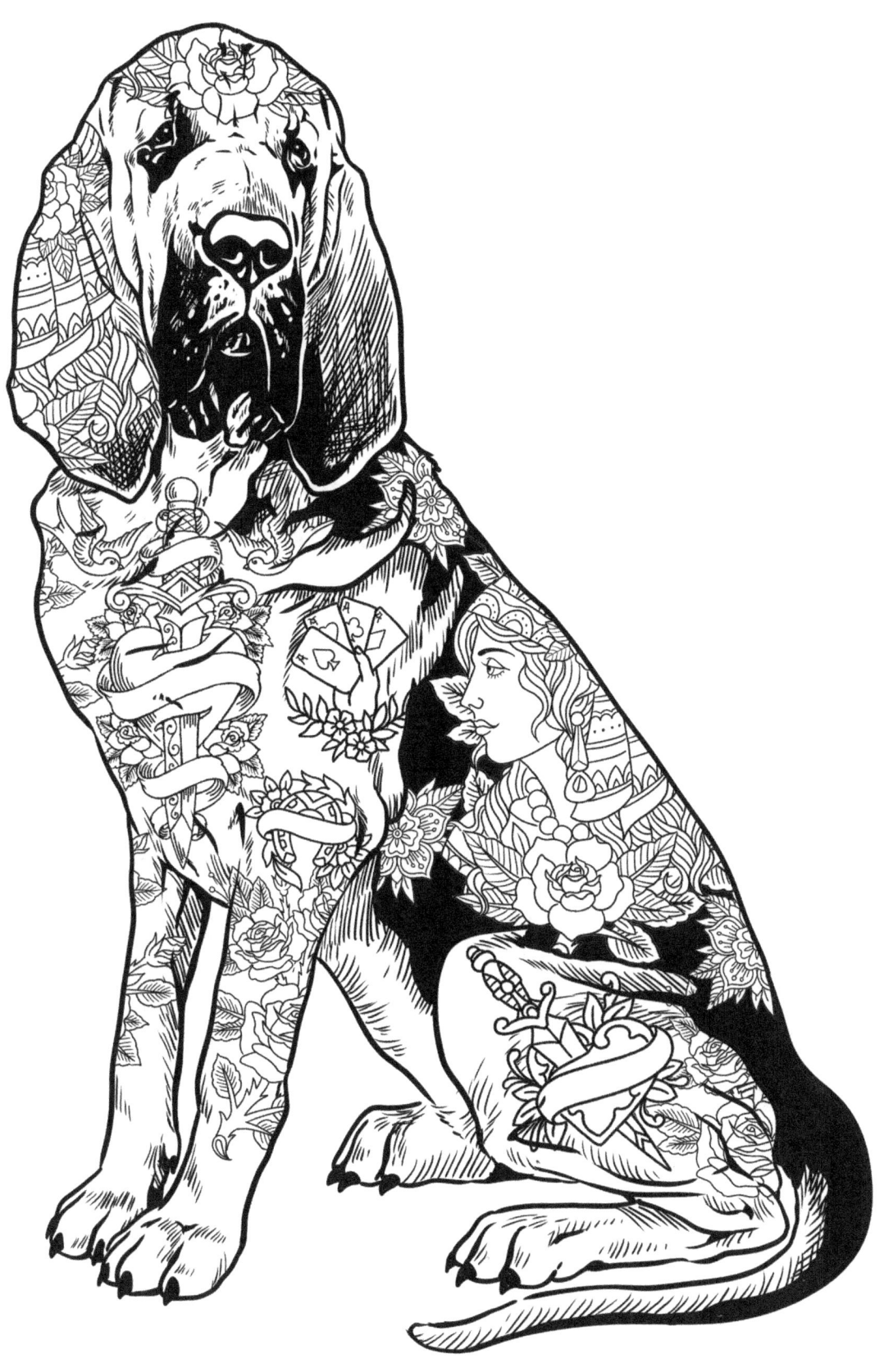

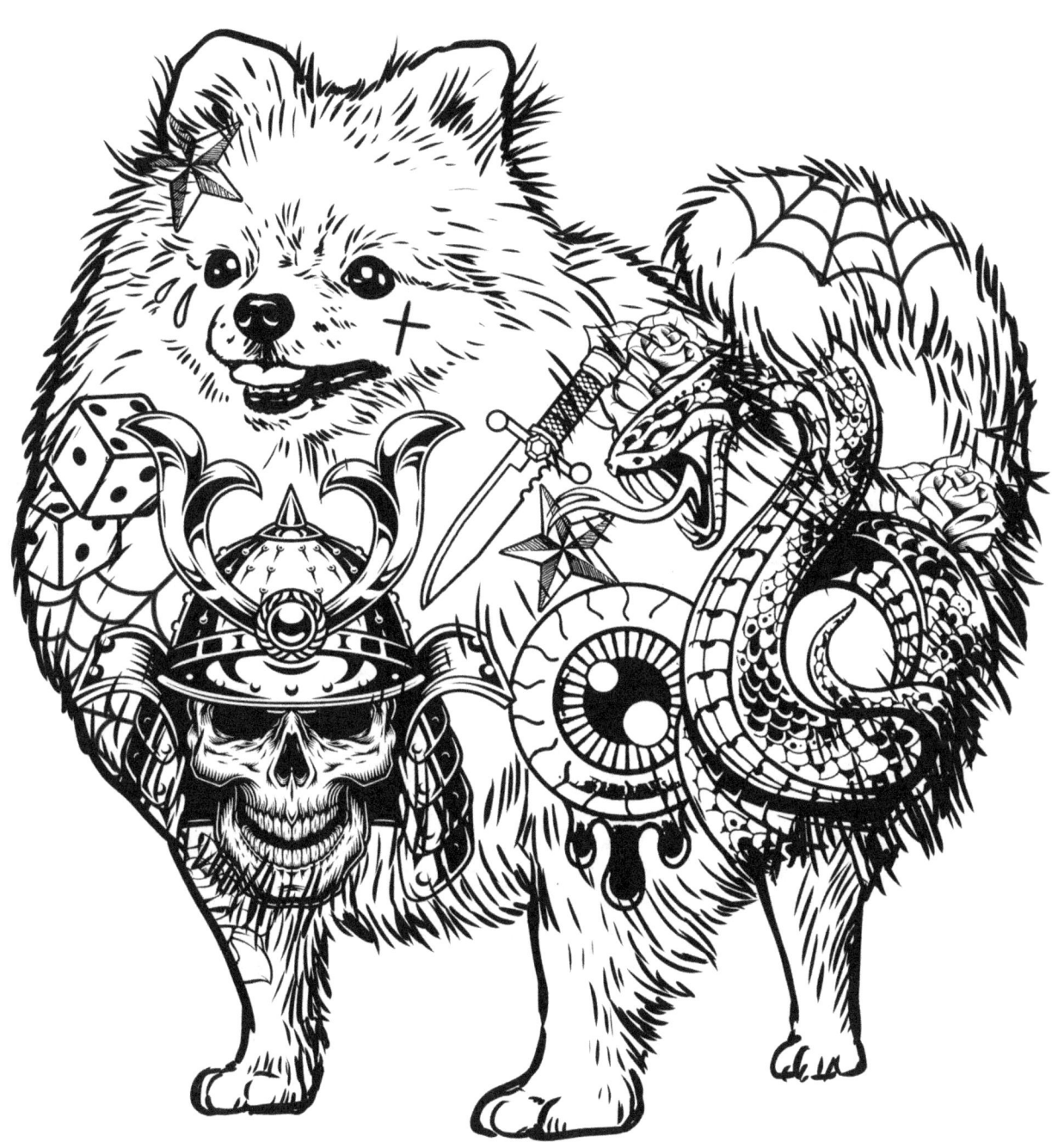

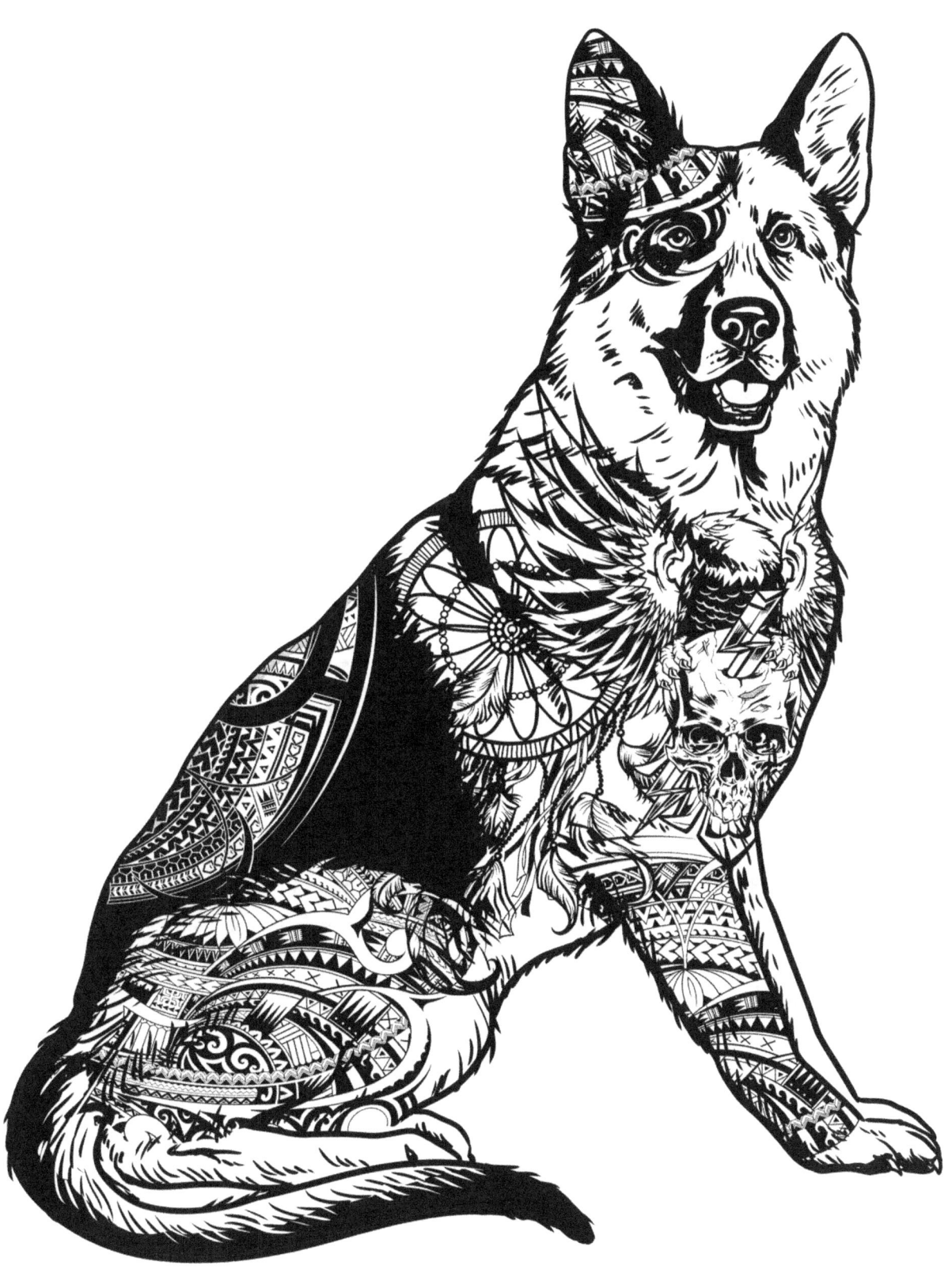

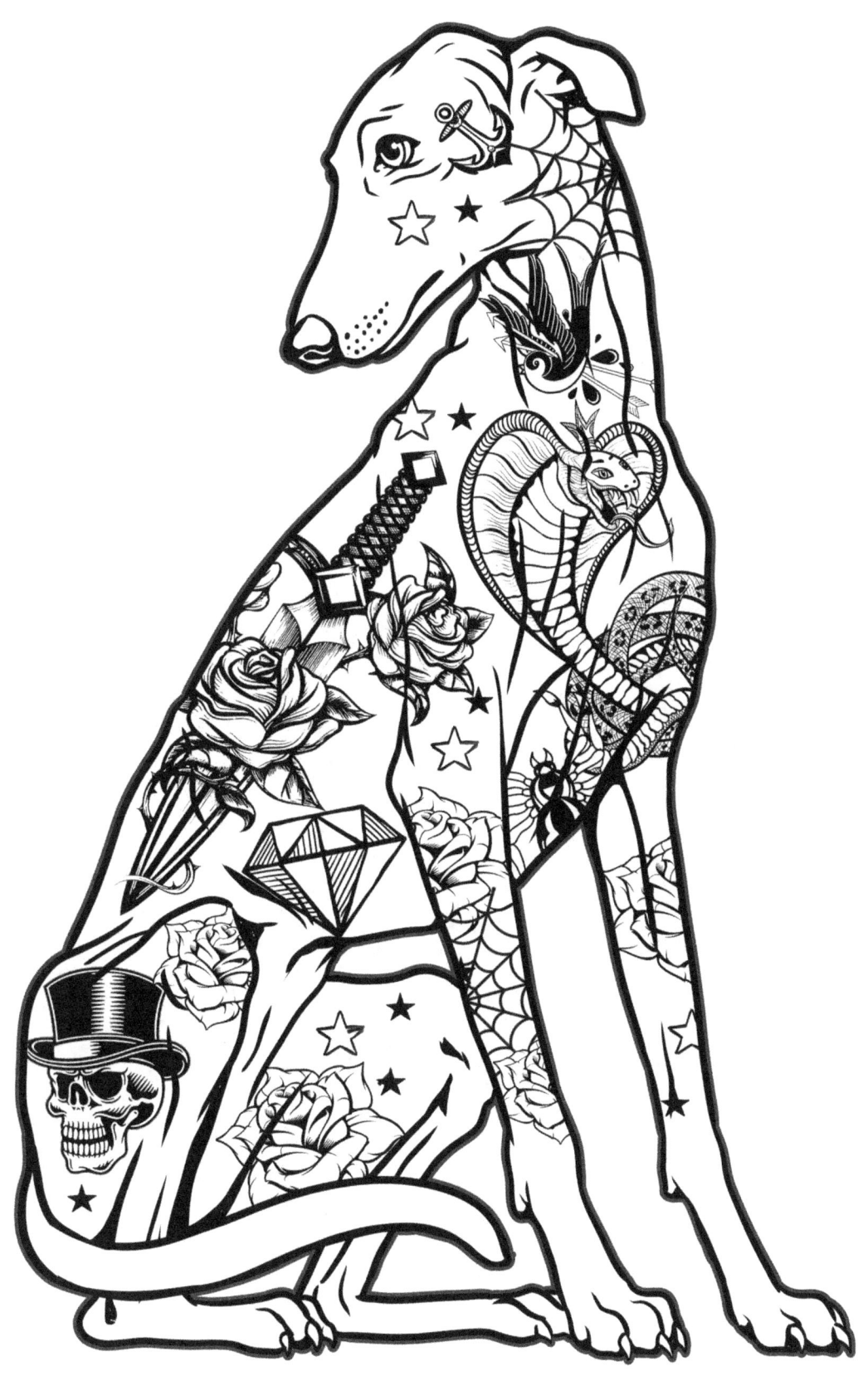

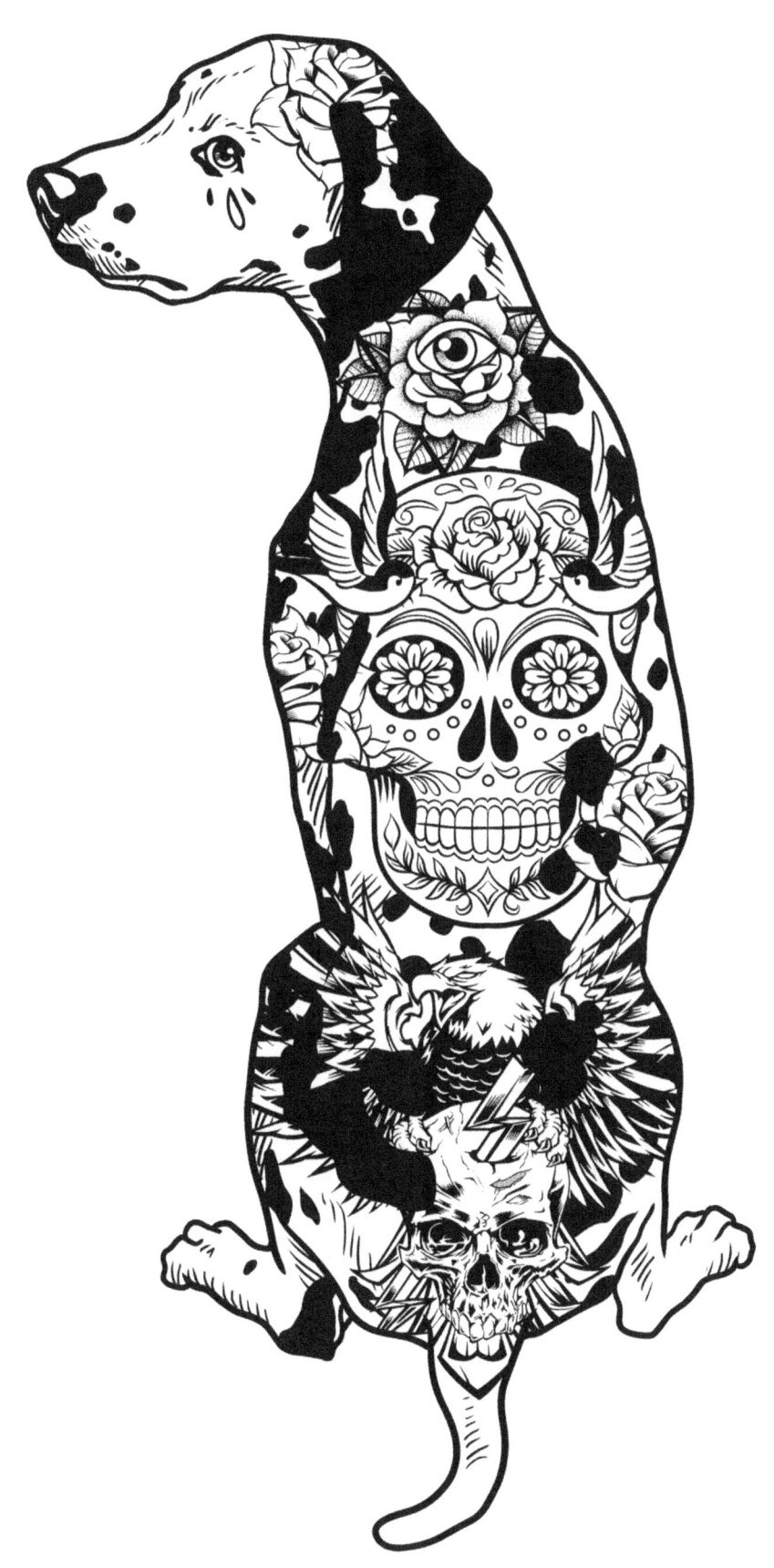

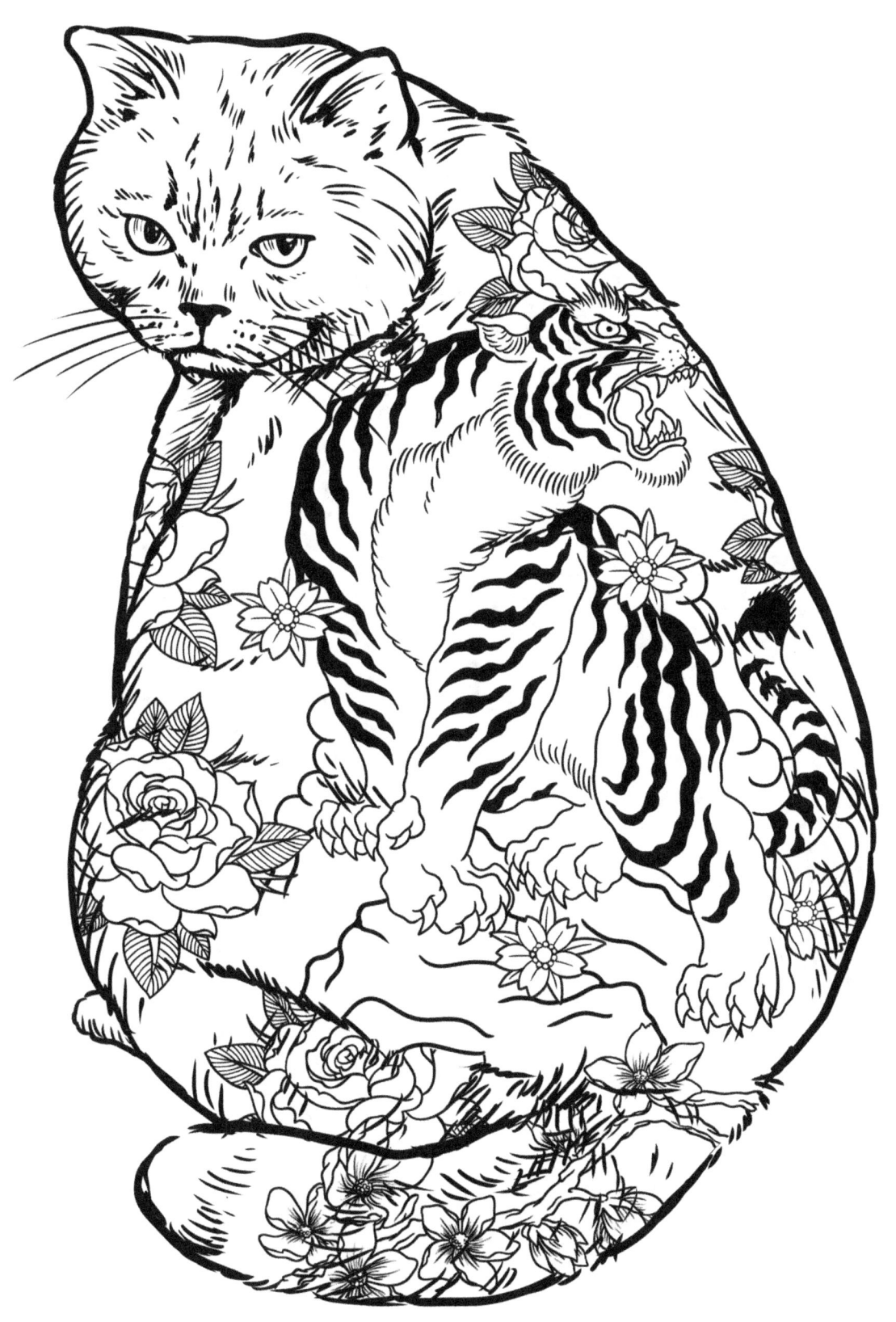

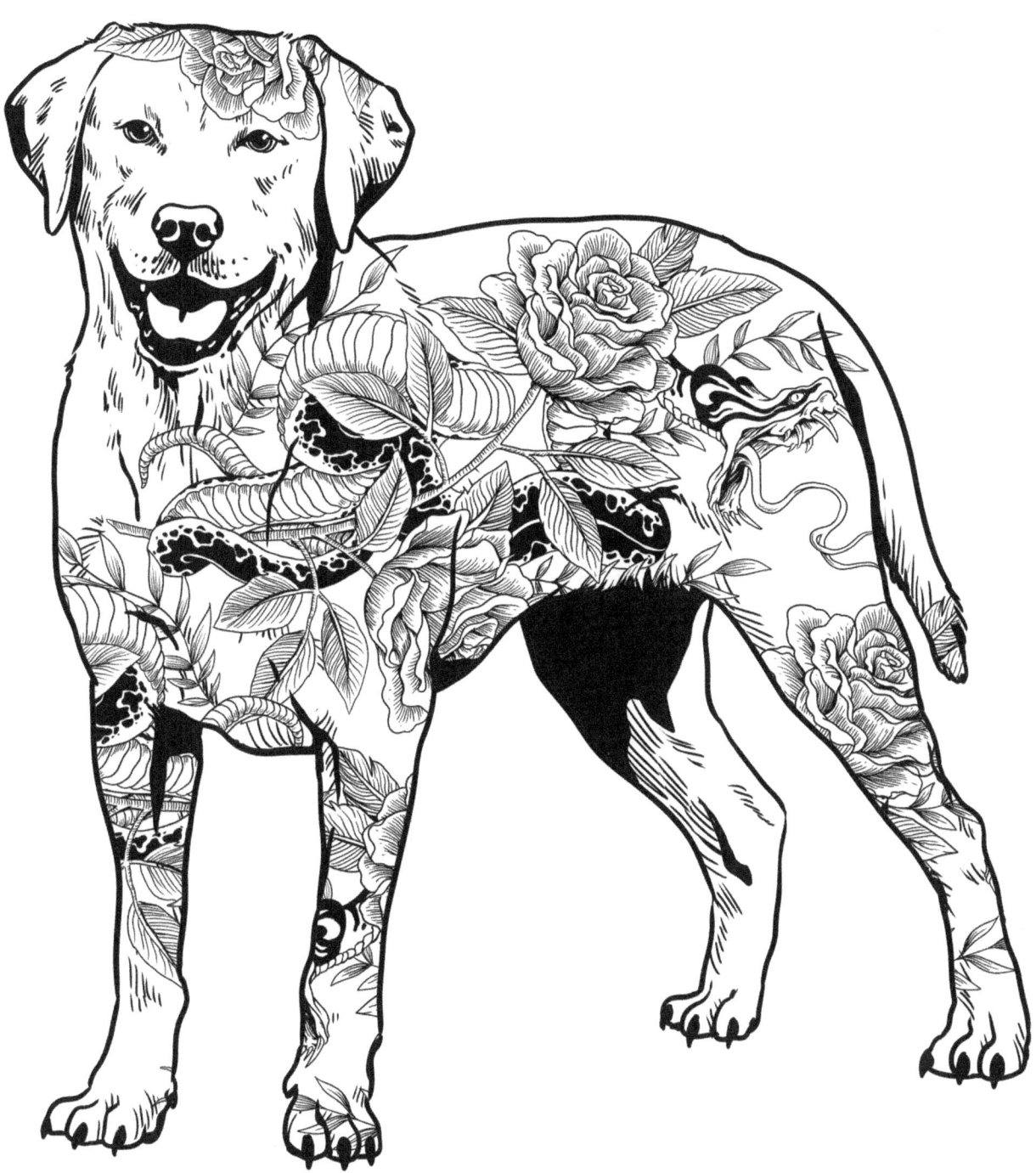

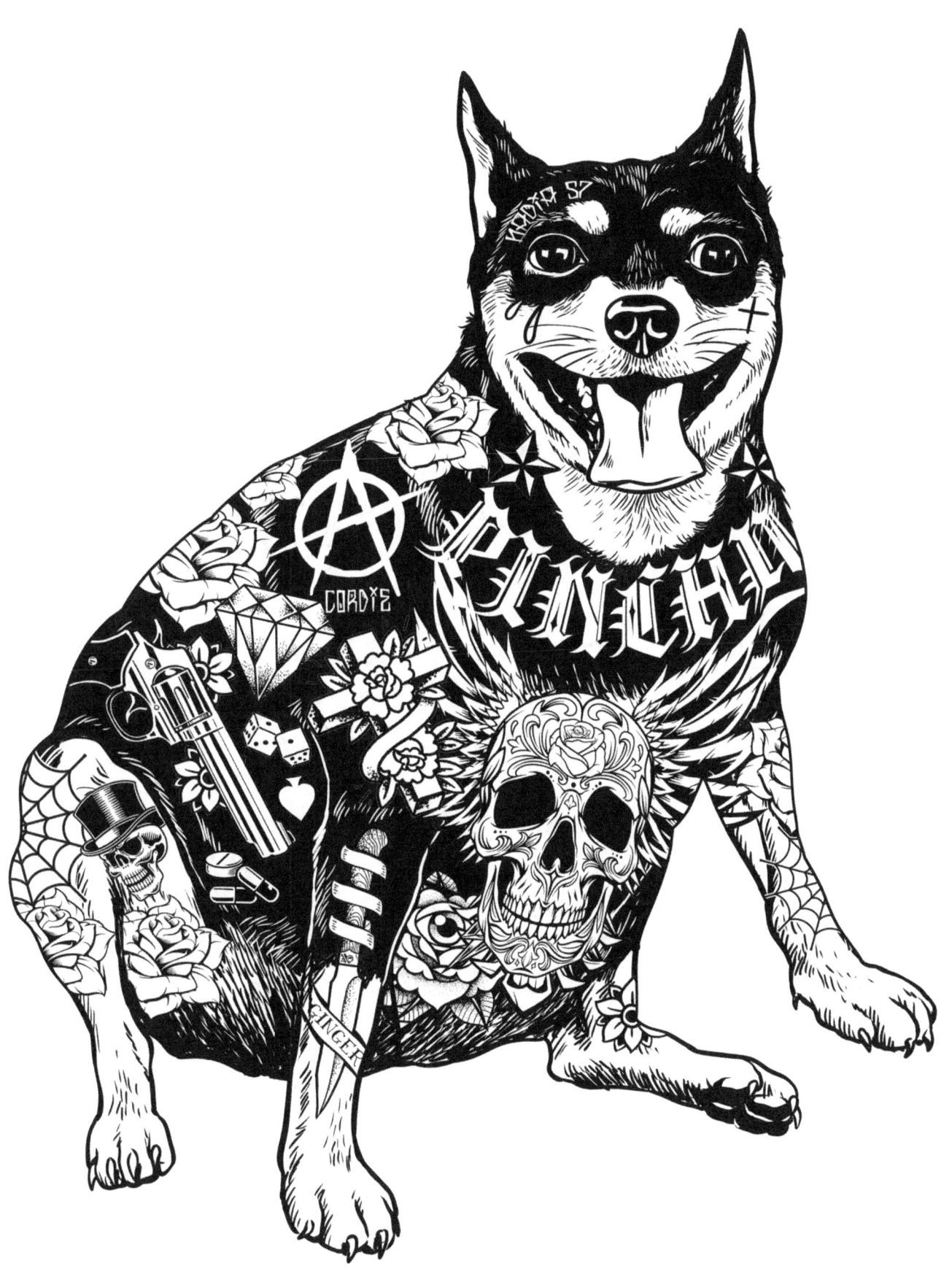

www.ingramcontent.com/pod-product-compliance
Lightning Source LLC
Chambersburg PA
CBHW080533220526

45465CB00006B/2693